Little People, BIG DREAMS™

FREDDIE MERCURY

Written by
Maria Isabel Sánchez Vegara

Illustrated by
Ruby Taylor

Frances Lincoln
Children's Books

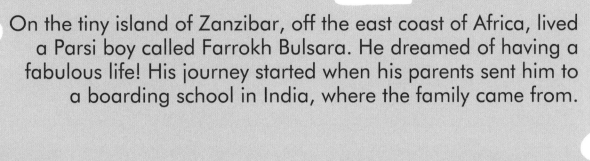

On the tiny island of Zanzibar, off the east coast of Africa, lived a Parsi boy called Farrokh Bulsara. He dreamed of having a fabulous life! His journey started when his parents sent him to a boarding school in India, where the family came from.

In school, Farrokh took piano lessons. Soon he was repeating any melody he heard on the radio, especially if it was rock 'n' roll.

But it was at choir where he showed he also had a natural talent for singing.

While most kids have 20 teeth, Farrokh had four more.
They took up a lot of space inside his mouth ...

... but he believed that these teeth helped him reach the highest and lowest pitches of his favorite songs.

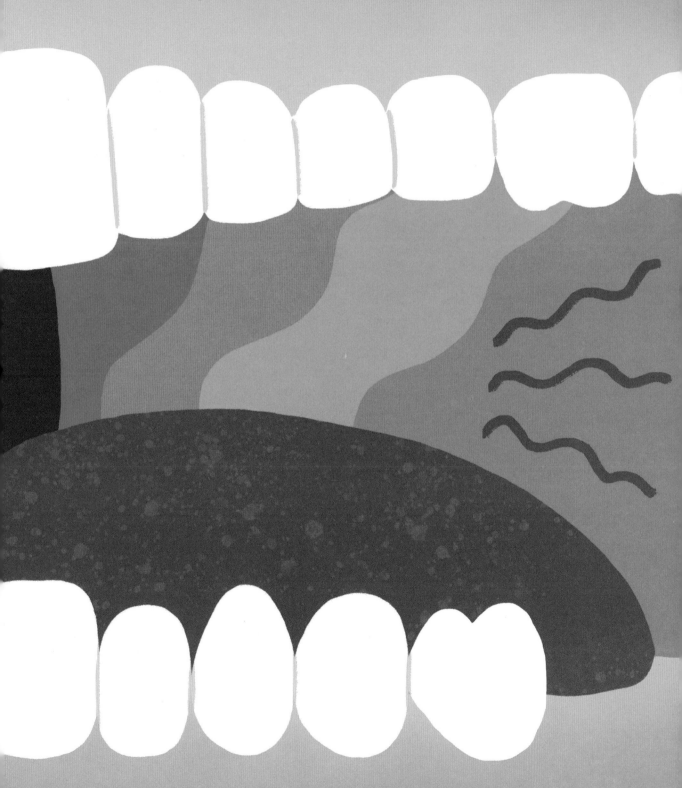

By the time he was 12, Farrokh had formed a band
with some friends and started calling himself Freddie.
He was obsessed with any new music coming from England,
and being a rock star was all he could think about.

After graduating from school, he went back
to Zanzibar. Only two years later, his family
left the island and moved to England.

Suddenly, Freddie found himself in London,
one of the coolest cities for a young musician like him.

He studied graphic design and sold second-hand clothes at a trendy market. There, he hung out with Roger and Brian, members of a band called Smile. They were looking for a singer. It was the chance Freddie had been waiting for!

SECOND HAND

Last to join them was a guy called John, and once the band
was completed, Freddie convinced them to change their name
to Queen. He also took a new last name from the lyrics of one
of his songs, and Farrokh Bulsara became Freddie Mercury.

Freddie always knew he was a star, but the world only seemed to agree with him after Queen's third album. It launched the band to fame. Next came "Bohemian Rhapsody," an exciting song that mixed opera with rock. It was genius!

All four members of Queen were talented composers. Still, no matter who wrote a song, Freddie always gave it his all, electrifying the lyrics with his voice.

As a result, their tunes became instant classics, and one in particular is now an anthem at any sporting event.

On stage, Freddie gave everyone goosebumps—even people standing at the very back. He performed at a charity concert that almost half of the planet watched live on television.

Years later, it was voted as the greatest show in rock history!

Even though he was admired by millions, Freddie felt that the only ones who truly knew him were his first and only girlfriend, Mary, and his ten beloved cats. Then, one day, he met Jim, and they were together forever after.

When doctors told him he had AIDS, an illness that had taken many friends away, Freddie stopped touring but he didn't give up singing. Instead, he recorded the most beautiful song to say goodbye: "The Show Must Go On."

Still, it wasn't really a goodbye. Not at all! Because little Freddie—one of the greatest performers of all time— keeps electrifying our hearts with his music, encouraging us to live a fabulous life ... a life as fabulous as we want it to be!

FREDDIE MERCURY

(Born 1946 – Died 1991)

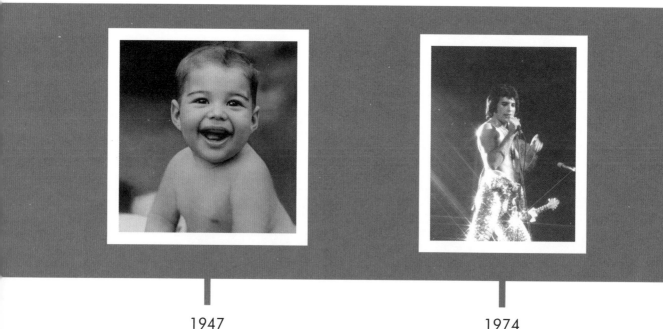

1947

1974

Farrokh Bulsara was born in Zanzibar (now Tanzania) to Parsi-Indian parents. As a child, he was sent to St. Peter's boarding school in Maharashtra, India, where he was nicknamed Freddie. It was clear from a young age that he was musically talented: he took piano lessons and had an impressive four-octave vocal range. After school he returned to Zanzibar but, due to political unrest in the country, he moved to England with his family in 1964. Farrokh met guitarist Brian May and drummer Roger Taylor and became lead singer of their band, Smile. When John Deacon joined the group, they became Queen. Around the same time, he changed his legal name to Freddie Mercury, inspired by the line "Mother mercury, look what they've done to me," from their song, "My Fairy King."

1976   1986

Their third album, *Sheer Heart Attack*, was a massive success and their song
"Bohemian Rhapsody" spent nine weeks at the top of the British charts. By the
early 1980s, Queen was an international phenomenon! Freddie commanded
the audience in exciting outfits, such as a striped leotard or his famous yellow
military jacket. At Queen's unforgettable performance at Live Aid in
July 1985, around 75,000 people sang along to their songs, with billions
more watching on television. Freddie was diagnosed with AIDS but he
carried on singing until he eventually had to stop. He died the day after he
announced his illness to the world. Many rock legends performed at a huge
tribute concert that was held in his memory. To this day, Freddie still lives in
the hearts of millions of music fans as one of the greatest stars ever to shine.

Want to find out more about **Freddie Mercury?**

Have a read of this great book:

The Extraordinary Life of Freddie Mercury by Michael Lee Richardson

Brimming with creative inspiration, how-to projects, and useful information to enrich your everyday life, quarto.com is a favourite destination for those pursuing their interests and passions.

Text © 2023 Maria Isabel Sánchez Vegara. Illustrations © 2023 Ruby Taylor.
Original concept of the series by Maria Isabel Sánchez Vegara, published by Alba Editorial, S.L.U.
"Little People, BIG DREAMS" and "Pequeña & Grande" are trademarks of Alba Editorial S.L.U.
and/or Beautifool Couple S.L.
First Published in the UK in 2023 by Frances Lincoln Children's Books, an imprint of The Quarto Group.
100 Cummings Center, Suite 265D, Beverly, MA 01915, USA
T +1 978-282-9590 www.Quarto.com

This book is not authorised, licensed or approved by the estate of Freddie Mercury.
Any faults are the publisher's, who will be happy to rectify for future printings.
A catalogue record for this book is available from the British Library.
ISBN 978-0-7112-7108-1
Set in Futura BT.

Published by Peter Marley • Designed by Sasha Moxon
Commissioned by Lucy Menzies • Edited by Rachel Robinson and Lucy Menzies
Production by Nikki Ingram
Manufactured in Guangdong, China CC092022
1 3 5 7 9 8 6 4 2

Photographic acknowledgements (pages 28-29, from left to right): 1. 1947 , may , ZANZIBAR , TANZANIA : The celebrated singer and songwriter FREDDIE MERCURY (1946 - 1991) when was a child aged 8 months © Archivio GBB via Alamy Stock Photos. 2. Queen 6/77 Freddie Mercury © Chris Walter via Getty Images. 3. Queen, photo session for 'Music Life' magazine, in the garden of Hotel Pacific Tokyo on their Night At The Opera Japan tour, Tokyo, Japan, 21 March 1976. L-R John Deacon, Roger Taylor, Brian May, Freddie Mercury. It was the band's second Japanese tour. © Koh Hasebe/Shinko Music via Getty Images. 4. Freddie Mercury, of the pop band Queen, performing on stage during the Live Aid concert. © PA Images via Alamy Stock Photos

Collect the *Little People*, **BIG DREAMS**™ series:

FRIDA KAHLO	COCO CHANEL	MAYA ANGELOU	AMELIA EARHART	AGATHA CHRISTIE	MARIE CURIE	ROSA PARKS	AUDREY HEPBURN

EMMELINE PANKHURST	ELLA FITZGERALD	ADA LOVELACE	JANE AUSTEN	GEORGIA O'KEEFFE	HARRIET TUBMAN	ANNE FRANK	MOTHER TERESA

JOSEPHINE BAKER	L. M. MONTGOMERY	JANE GOODALL	SIMONE DE BEAUVOIR	MUHAMMAD ALI	STEPHEN HAWKING	MARIA MONTESSORI	VIVIENNE WESTWOOD

MAHATMA GANDHI	DAVID BOWIE	WILMA RUDOLPH	DOLLY PARTON	BRUCE LEE	RUDOLF NUREYEV	ZAHA HADID	MARY SHELLEY

MARTIN LUTHER KING JR.	DAVID ATTENBOROUGH	ASTRID LINDGREN	EVONNE GOOLAGONG	BOB DYLAN	ALAN TURING	BILLIE JEAN KING	GRETA THUNBERG

JESSE OWENS	JEAN-MICHEL BASQUIAT	ARETHA FRANKLIN	CORAZON AQUINO	PELÉ	ERNEST SHACKLETON	STEVE JOBS	AYRTON SENNA

LOUISE BOURGEOIS	ELTON JOHN	JOHN LENNON	PRINCE	CHARLES DARWIN	CAPTAIN TOM MOORE	HANS CHRISTIAN ANDERSEN	STEVIE WONDER

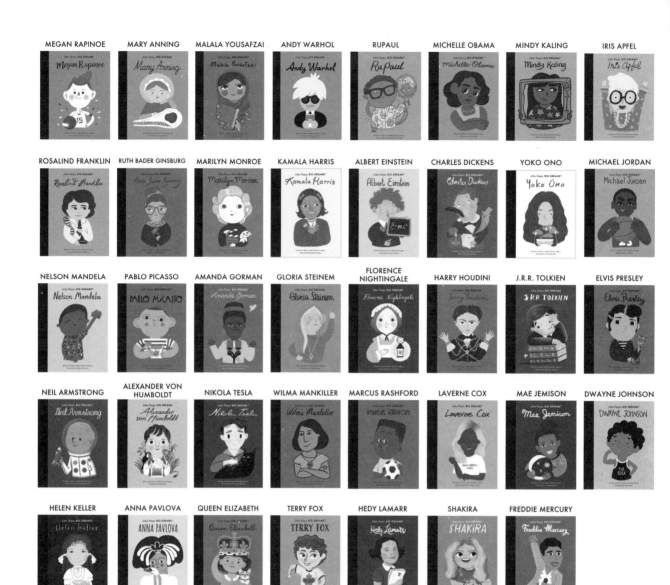

MEGAN RAPINOE	MARY ANNING	MALALA YOUSAFZAI	ANDY WARHOL	RUPAUL	MICHELLE OBAMA	MINDY KALING	IRIS APFEL
ROSALIND FRANKLIN	RUTH BADER GINSBURG	MARILYN MONROE	KAMALA HARRIS	ALBERT EINSTEIN	CHARLES DICKENS	YOKO ONO	MICHAEL JORDAN
NELSON MANDELA	PABLO PICASSO	AMANDA GORMAN	GLORIA STEINEM	FLORENCE NIGHTINGALE	HARRY HOUDINI	J.R.R. TOLKIEN	ELVIS PRESLEY
NEIL ARMSTRONG	ALEXANDER VON HUMBOLDT	NIKOLA TESLA	WILMA MANKILLER	MARCUS RASHFORD	LAVERNE COX	MAE JEMISON	DWAYNE JOHNSON
HELEN KELLER	ANNA PAVLOVA	QUEEN ELIZABETH	TERRY FOX	HEDY LAMARR	SHAKIRA	FREDDIE MERCURY	

ACTIVITY BOOKS

STICKER ACTIVITY BOOK

COLORING BOOK

LITTLE ME, BIG DREAMS JOURNAL

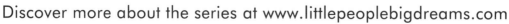

Discover more about the series at www.littlepeoplebigdreams.com